Most Guys Are Clueless

What Every Woman Wishes Her Man Knew!
What Every Man Needs To Know!

David Gordon

Most Guys Are Clueless

Copyright © 2009, 2021 David Gordon

ISBN: 978-1-935125-46-4

The information contained herein is true to the best of the reporter's knowledge, relying on the veracity of the parties involved. Only the names have been changed, to protect... the guilty.

Printed in the USA and UK on acid-free paper.

To purchase additional books go to:
Amazon.com

Rp

Robertson Publishing™
www.RobertsonPublishing.com

Watching my father navigate through the maze of dating and relationships after the death of my mother has been interesting, to say the least. What does one say to an older man who experiences the trials and tribulations of dating for the first time? My father has thrown himself wholeheartedly into the pursuit of new relationships armed with the experiences of a relationship that lasted over thirty years. He has melded his musings and advice into this book which is valuable for anyone, male or female, to read. It may make you laugh, and it may make you think, "I can do that!" It can't hurt to try, right?

— Nina Gordon

Introduction

I'm 73 years old. I've been in monogamous relationships for just over 48 of those years. One was a 30-year relationship which included a 27-year marriage. It ended when she lost her courageous battle with breast cancer.

There was a subsequent 5-year relationship (3-year marriage) that didn't work out. (Her very best friend supports my version, so I'm good!) There were a couple of exhilarating but relatively brief true loves, and a number of friendships and lovers that I cherish.

Of the women that I count as having forged a relationship with during the twenty-four years since my first love's passing, I'm in contact with virtually all. And as we've developed relationships of all sorts, what I've heard when they share their frustrations is that most guys are clueless, and have no idea how to relate to a woman.

The ladies tell me to write a book about what I've learned. Here it is.

It will help you enrich your relationships.

Thanks to Carol, Diane, Ellyn, Jan, Leslie, Linda, Lori, Marcey, Marianne, Meradith, Nan, Sally, Sharon, Sheri, Vicky, Nina, Ted, Danny, Natalie, Ellen, Julius and Rose.

You can contact me at: dngbiz@aol.com

David

The L Word

Be careful when you use it. Do not bandy it about. Cherish it.

When you do tell her that you love her, you'd better mean it, and that has implications.

Remember that you can love someone like you love a friend or a sibling, but when you tell your lady that you "love" her... you're telling her that you are "in love" with her. She'd captured your heart.

Gifts

Give them.

They don't have to be expensive.

Little notes left for them in unexpected places are appreciated.

Flowers are big. Make sure you know what kind she likes. Bring them frequently, for no reason other than you want her to enjoy them.

Candies are good, too. Chocolates are "medicinal" and reputedly an aphrodisiac. Even stopping by the local "See's Candies" or equivalent to put three or four of her favorites in a little bag is good.

Cards are wonderful too. My late wife taught me to look in the card sections and buy ones that I like when I see them. Keep an inventory that you can share at the appropriate time with your honey.

I like to give earrings. They don't have to be 2 carat solitaires. It's the thought that counts.

I also like to give gift certificates for a professional massage. They really appreciate the thought.

There are also little things, thoughtful actions that go a long way. Cook dinner for her, do her laundry, make the bed, pick up after yourself, fill her car up with gas; without having to be asked. These count as gifts, too.

A special sort of gift, part of the intimacy of a relationship is an unexpected hug or kiss or loving caress.

"Yes, Dear"

Practice saying it. And mean it. This comes from the heart. Don't be smug or flip.

Make Her Happy

If you love her, you will do anything and everything in your power to make her happy.

Communication

Open, honest communication is critical. Trust is critical. Try to be as communicative as you can. Listen well. Make sure you have her attention and eye contact when discussing important issues.

One of my rules is to never go to bed angry. If we were unable to reach an accord, and it's way past our sleep time, we always agreed to a time to reopen the conversation.

Also agree that disagreement does not preclude intimacy and sex.

This is like your kids in a way. You always love them, but sometimes you hate their behavior. Same thing here, you love her, you just may not like her behavior at the moment.

Another critical rule is that there is no topic that is off the table for discussion. Talk about anything and everything.

Sex

Rule #1: Make her happy.

There are no other rules. Do this and you are golden.

In case you hadn't noticed, there are some biological and physiological differences between the sexes.

Generally speaking, you are going to get yours, have your orgasm. It might be in a short time, or it might take a while, but pretty much you're going to have yours.

Women are different. Some require more stimulation than others to have an orgasm. Few can have one from penetration. Most require clitoral stimulation. Fingers or your mouth work really well. Many can have an orgasm from stimulation of their G-spot.

Most women want, need and enjoy extended foreplay. They also want and enjoy holding, cuddling, caressing after sex.

If you haven't figured this one out, for some background theory, there are many books on the subject; shelves of them are available at your local bookstore or online. Bet the local library might even have a few, too.

Communication is important. Talk to your lady.

Ask her what feels best. How does she please herself? Ask to watch. You might find out she likes that.

Ask her what her fantasies are. This is not necessarily a conversation in bed, although it can be fun during sex. It makes for interesting conversation at dinner, via e-mail or IMing, over then phone when you're apart or just snuggling on the couch.

It's your responsibility to find out what works for your partner, what she likes, when she likes it and how she likes it. If you take the time to help her have as many orgasms as she would like or can handle, I will guarantee that she will want to make you happy.

If you need religious justification, The Kabala, the mystic Jewish teachings that seem to be in vogue among some Hollywood celebrities, instructs men to pleasure their woman first.

In her book, Bonk, Mary Roach discusses a Masters and Johnston book titled Homosexuality in Perspective which was a study of sex in pairs of adults, both heterosexual and gay/lesbian.

The study showed that the gay/lesbian pairs had the best sex because they took their time. They played with their partners to create the maximum arousal and pleasure. They were turned on my making their partners happy. There was more communication about what was pleasing and felt good.

Make it your pleasure to make sure that she gets as much pleasure as she wants, and you'll have great sex too!

The Four Chemistries

I wondered about why some relationships don't work out. Have you ever thought or heard someone say something like the following... "I really love him/her. We communicate well and the sex is great, but it's just not working."

I figured out that there are four chemistries or elements that make a relationship.

Great Friends: You have to be great friends. People treat friends with great concern, courtesy, warmth. Sometimes they treat their friends better than their family or loved ones. Friends share intimacies. Friends can talk about anything.

You have to be able to talk about anything. One of the rules is that there is no topic that is off the table for conversation. And you must master the ability to disagree and not argue.

Great Sex: You have to have great sex. Pretty self-explanatory. You both have to enjoy the physical melding. See the chapter on sex.

Great Intimacy: Intimacy is not sex. Intimacy is the ethereal "being in love," touching, being with, holding hands, snuggling, soft kisses, sharing being lost in their eyes, walking hand in hand or arm in arm... and the like. You can have sex without intimacy, but it will not be as wonderful and rewarding. You might have intimacy in the relationship long before you get skin to skin.

Lifestyle Congruence: This is the chemistry that causes the biggest problem between two people. I think it's the one that causes the most disconnects.

Similar values and morals are important. Your life-styles need to be compatible. Does that mean mirror images? Of course not, however, there needs to be some congruency and mutual agreement so that you can be and live together.

Some examples:

> She's a vegetarian, and he loves his steaks. As long as she doesn't mind that he's a carnivore, no problem. If she's militant about vegetarianism, this will not work, will it?

> He likes his liquor, and she's in recovery, going to several 12 step meetings a week. See the challenge?

> He plays a lot of golf. She does not. If she's ok with the time he takes playing, and he doesn't care that she does not share that activity, no problem. But, if he wants her with him or she objects to the time he spends apart from her, this is an issue.

> He's a political conservative, successful business person. She's a left wing, liberal, socialist artsy, woman. If they can agree to disagree with out arguing and respect each other's beliefs, no problem. If not, this is not going to work.

Her home is spotless and immaculate. His residence is a pigsty. As long as they are at her place or out and about, there is no issue. She can't abide being at his place and knows they are never going to be able to cohabit. As long as the status quo is that they don't go to his place, it works. If the relationship is going to escalate to the next step, something is going to have to change.

Here's a personal one. My favorite movies are considered "chick flicks"... boy meets girl, boy loses girl, boy finds girl and they live happily ever after. When movies have disturbing themes or images, those images tend to stay with me, and I don't like the recurring images. So, my late wife had some friends that she would go with to movies that she wanted to see.

Get my drift? Differences are not deadly to the relationship if accord and mutual agreement are reached about the differences in lifestyle.

In Passionate Marriage, David Schnarch uses a term "differentiation." My interpretation of this is... the ability of one of the significant others to acquiesce to their partner's wishes without feeling demeaned.

For example...

Your lady says she's going to the mall to shop and asks if you would like to go with her.

- You should be able to say yes, enjoy the

time with her, carry her purchases without feeling like "real men don't' go shopping."

• You should also be able to tell her that you'd really like to watch the playoff game without her feeling rejected and hurt.

Personally, I think that if one takes one other's happiness to heart and are willing to compromise without feeling that you've giving up part of yourself... one can make the relationship work.

Last Words

It's all about making her feel special and cherished; doing the little things that show you care; having honest, open communication; and an unswerving commitment to your relationship and to her.

Suggested Reading

Read these. If something strikes home, share it with your honey. She will appreciate it.

Passionate Marriage by David Schnarch

Sex on the Brain by Daniel Amen

The Seven Levels of Intimacy by Matthew Kelley

The Care and Feeding of Marriage by Dr. Laura Schlessinger

The Four Agreements by Don Miguel Ruiz

Notes

www.ingramcontent.com/pod-product-compliance
Lightning Source LLC
Chambersburg PA
CBHW040348060426
42445CB00029B/42